YORKTOWN

YORKTOWN

Growing Up

In Small-Town Iowa

Richard B. Ulmer Jr.

News Ink Books

News Ink Books

© 2012 by Richard B. Ulmer Jr.
ISBN 978-0-9849036-2-7
Autobiography/Memoir/Childhood

Original Illustrations by Lynne D. Schneider
Cover Design by Carlos Velez
Interior Design by Terry Bradshaw

www.newsinkbooks.com
10 9 8 7 6 5 4 3 2 1

Contents

Introduction   vii

CHAPTER 1   The Heyday   1
CHAPTER 2   Mac's World   7
CHAPTER 3   A Lawless Society   13
CHAPTER 4   Endless Summer   17
CHAPTER 5   Town Tableau   23
CHAPTER 6   Monochrome   33
CHAPTER 7   Mass Communicating   37
CHAPTER 8   Outside Lands   41
CHAPTER 9   Black Gold   45
CHAPTER 10   Lesser Creatures   51

Contents

CHAPTER 11	As You Sow	55
CHAPTER 12	Out of Hannover	59
CHAPTER 13	The Call	65
CHAPTER 14	All Above Average	69
CHAPTER 15	Two-Room School	75
CHAPTER 16	Ulmer Ultimatums	81
CHAPTER 17	In a Strange Land	87
CHAPTER 18	Hamburger 100 Ways	91
CHAPTER 19	Tornado!	97
CHAPTER 20	The Aftermath	101
CHAPTER 21	Too Tough to Die?	105

Postscript		109
Acknowledgements		111
About the Author		113

Introduction

"Daddy, tell me about Yorktown."

Years ago at bedtime here in Northern California, my daughter, Rikki, would ask for stories about the Iowa hamlet where I grew up. It was our Oz, I suppose. Recently as Rikki prepared to leave for college, I found myself jotting down the stories we had shared of those days in the 1960s.

Today, a half-century on, it is difficult to envision an America where children roamed streets freely, doors went unlocked and no police patrolled. But that America existed in more than Norman Rockwell illustrations. It existed in Yorktown.

This small book about a small town in southwestern Iowa is for Rikki. Perhaps you too will find it of interest.
—Richard B. Ulmer Jr.
San Francisco, California
Fall 2012

CHAPTER I

The Heyday

IN 1898, OUR FUTURE HOMETOWN was an unnamed spot on the map. As the town prepared to incorporate, citizens were asked to pick a name. Their choices: Loy (after its first postmaster) or Yorktown.

The closest town to the south faced a similar naming dilemma. Unable to decide between two alternatives, its founders flipped a coin—which landed on edge. Hence the town's name: Coin.

The populace of our town opted for conventionality. It joined the Yorktowns (cities, towns, and hamlets) in seventeen other United States. Not to mention countless

Yorktown streets, neighborhoods, schools, and shopping malls to come—as well as an aircraft carrier.

Most of these Yorktowns—including Page County, Iowa's—descended directly from Yorktown, Virginia, site of an ignominious British defeat in the Revolutionary War. Thus continues the fine American tradition of rubbing it in.

Yorktown of Iowa maintained its conventionality in selection of street names. Main, Washington, Jefferson, Lincoln, Second, Third, and Fourth had been platted in 1882. Not that most residents ever knew the name of any street save Main. No street signs were posted, no houses numbered. The only address an incoming letter required: "John Doe, Yorktown, Iowa."

Visitors to town might be guided by landmarks such as house colors. But that proved unhelpful, as the vast majority of structures were a sterile white. Alternatively, one could simply follow the sign from State Highway 2, reach town, and then ask after their destination. From the beginning, everyone in Yorktown knew everyone else.

Set in the rolling hills of Iowa's southwest corner, Yorktown's nearest neighbors to the east and west were Clarinda and Shenandoah (another Virginia allusion). Both straddled Highway 2. Yorktown, in contrast, elected to situate itself a half-mile off the road, thereby missing travelers on what became a two-lane blacktop. This was because the Humeston and Shenandoah Railroad ran south of the highway, and Yorktown's founders placed their bet on steel wheels over rubber. Unhappily, the railroad spur was short-lived. The highway prevailed, and Yorktown became commercially stranded—a small town for however long it might survive.

It survives today—barely. Yorktown had a population of eighty-five at the 2010 census. More than a century after the town's founding, satellite images of the little spot look very much like the yellowed plat map from the 1800s, a tiny trapezoid of perpendicular streets among swirling contours of farm fields.

The Highway 2 towns of Clarinda (2010 population: 5,572) and Shenandoah (pop. 5,150) thrived by comparison. Indeed, each boasts a legitimate musical claim to fame.

Clarinda is birthplace of Glenn Miller, the Big Band Era's leading figure. Miller's lushly orchestrated numbers—"Moonlight Serenade," "Chattanooga Choo Choo," "In the Mood," "(I've Got a Gal in) Kalamazoo"—were (and are) a pleasure to hear. This made him unpopular with jazz purists (Deadheads of their time and genre) who insisted on inaccessible improvisation. The public disagreed. The Glenn Miller Orchestra scored seventy Top Ten hits between 1938 and 1942. When the U.S. entered World War II, Glenn joined the military and formed what critics regard as his finest band. On December 15, 1944, his plane went down over the English Channel while touring for the troops. Neither plane nor body was ever found.

Shenandoah also nurtured musical talent. The Everly Brothers—Don and Phil—got started on their parents' live radio show on KMA and KFNF in the 1940s. Shortly after leaving "Shen," the Everlys began topping charts with countrified rock & roll such as "Bye Bye Love," "All I Have to Do Is Dream," and "Cathy's Clown." They became one of only four acts inducted into both the Rock & Roll *and* Country Music halls of fame. (The other three: Elvis, Johnny Cash, and Brenda Lee.)

Meanwhile, no one famous—musical or otherwise—ever lived in Yorktown.

The town's heyday, to the extent it had one, was early on. Population peaked at 228 in the 1910 census. Businesses sprouted, including a lumberyard, blacksmith, hotel, and "opera house," where plays were performed. But no stage drama rivaled a particular moment of mayhem in local history. Three explosions at 3:30 A.M. on November 20, 1919, signaled one of the few newsworthy events ever to occur in Yorktown. Robbers had "blown" the Yorktown Savings Bank. According to an account in the *Clarinda Herald-Journal*, men of town hastily dressed, armed themselves, and "got out into the street" to exercise their Second Amendment rights.

"Seeing the jig was up," three (or maybe four; eyewitness accounts varied) robbers fled. One directed a shotgun blast at a Yorktownian but merely grazed him. Townspeople returned fire, wounding a robber. As his compatriots dragged him up the Main Street hill, he blubbered: "My God, Charlie, you are not going to leave me now!"

"Marks of bullets on the front of the bank, and in the tree in front show that some straight shooting was done," the *Herald-Journal* enthused.

The take was only $400 in nickels and $40 in pennies. Much of that was strewn on Main Street, to be collected by children and returned to the bank come light of day. Police radios remained uninvented, so Charlie and his confederates were never apprehended, and the golden age of bank-robbing continued until technology caught up in the 1930s. The Yorktown Savings Bank fell victim to the Great Depression in 1930.

Yorktown didn't make the news very often after that. But fantastical things were happening all around the place by the time we arrived. One just had to know where to look.

CHAPTER 2

Mac's World

BY 1960, YORKTOWN'S POPULATION had dwindled to 150. The railroad had long gone, and though the town did not die, it was no Clarinda. All that indicated a railroad ever existed was a phalanx of empty, twenty-foot-square concrete "sand bins" which made swell hideouts for kids. (Trains took on sand from the bins to sprinkle when rails became wet or steep.)

Snake Creek (invariably pronounced "crick") looped around the east and south edges of town and then off to join a larger Missouri River tributary we knew not where. The muddy stream was named for its serpentine path, Iowans being ever-clever. Absent a deluge, the crick ran no more than ten feet wide and two deep.

The streets of Yorktown were uncurbed asphalt with a dusting of gravel—the pea-size kind that embeds itself in knees during bicycle wrecks. Some forty houses spread over less than a square mile of gentle hills. The few remaining commercial buildings, of soft red brick, mostly stored farm machinery. Elegant elms studded town, but they would sadly soon succumb to the plague of Dutch elm disease. Vacant lots abounded, many populated by ponies and horses of indeterminate breed.

The salient civic feature of 1960s Yorktown was a bandstand smack in the middle of Main Street. A two-foot-high hexagon, the bandstand was ringed by cylindrical iron rails and had a towering flagpole. Locating a massive hunk of concrete in the center of a town's primary thoroughfare would have been a looming liability in another time and place. But Iowans were so good-natured, and Yorktown had so few assets, that no one ever sued.

No band had actually played on the stand in decades. It maintained socially redeeming value, however. The pole occasionally flew the Stars and Stripes, and it propped up an evergreen at Christmastime. Moreover, the bandstand was strategically situated at a 90-degree turn of what became a treacherous sledding hill in winter. Sledding meant dogfights. The skilled sledder sent his foe careening into a bloody encounter with the bandstand.

Commercial activity in 1960s Yorktown was limited to two places of business: Mac's and Eichhorsts'. Presumably each had a formal name, but they were nowhere displayed and no one ever used them. Eichhorsts'—on Main Street near the bandstand—was a combination general store and automotive garage. In those pre-Toyota days, motor vehicles required constant maintenance and frequent repair. An odometer rolling past 100,000 miles was a wonderment that friends and acquaintances were summoned to behold. So business was steady at Eichhorsts' garage.

Eichhorsts' store displayed a gift-wrapped chocolate bar for each Yorktown child at Christmastime. The store adjoined a compressed-sand croquet court lighted on summer nights. Formal croquet rules applied, although players donned faded farm overalls rather than dress whites.

While Eichhorsts' was appreciated, Mac's reigned as the center of Yorktown activity. And Marvin B. McElhiney was our town's leading citizen—postmaster, slaughterhouse proprietor, butcher, grocer, and possessor of the fire truck's keys.

Mac began the day sorting residents' mail into a wall of metal boxes in his store. Each box had a combination-dial lock embedded on front. Why was unclear, as the wall of boxes was readily accessible from the rear to anyone who wished to steal mail (though, of course, no Yorktownian ever so wished).

Next, Mac drove a faded red pickup truck two blocks south to his tiny slaughterhouse where he dispatched a cow or pig for a local farmer. Upon returning to his store, Mac cleaved and wrapped the decedent in white butcher paper stamped with names of cut and customer, then stored the packages in his frigid locker. All the while, a Winston dangled from Mac's lips, and his white apron became ever more speckled with carnage.

This butchery happened in the back of Mac's. The front, across from the postal boxes, was a child's garden of delights. Glass counters held candy bars—Milky Way, Snickers, Almond Joy—as long as a forearm and costing but a nickel. In another counter sat underappreciated fare like Cherry Mash and clove chewing gum. Nearby squatted jars of "penny candy" the likes of Jolly Rancher and red and black licorice whips.

Over beside the post office resided the pop machine. And "pop" was most decidedly the word for carbonated beverages in Yorktown, as in much of the Midwest. Not the "soda" of the coasts, or genericided "coke" of the South.

Mac's original pop machine was a horizontal model. Clasped by their crowns in iron bars, the bottles had to be manipulated like a flat Rubik's cube to guide the desired flavor to a slot that opened upon insertion of a dime. This was inefficient, so Mac later introduced a vertical pop machine that held bottles in a row behind a narrow swinging glass door. When a bottle was purchased, gravity rolled another in to replace it. This model too had a key deficiency: a wrongdoer could flip the cap from a bottle and drink for free through a straw. However, since Mac's machine sat indoors under his watchful eye, this did not prove problematic.

Almost all pop was heavily sugared, as in the formulae of modern-day Latin America. (Diet brands of the time, Tab and Fresca, were drinkable only by the masochistic.) Still, the Eichhorst boys could not get enough calories. They purchased a Pepsi from Mac's machine then funneled in a bag of Planter's salted peanuts before consuming the now-fizzing cocktail.

Lesser brands such as Canada Dry perched high on Mac's back shelves. These bottles were dust-covered, but their caps promised exotica like ginger ale, grapefruit, and tonic. In 1964, Mountain Dew was introduced to much acclaim (at least in Yorktown). It had a hillbilly theme then: "It'll tickle yore innards."

A pop bottle figured prominently in one of Mac's exploits. As he sorted mail on a spring morning, a pack of wolf-dogs set upon Kenny Eichhorst's spaniel, Sandy. These curs were associated with a new family on the east edge of town who'd emanated from Arkansas. The alpha male's jaws poised at Sandy's throat. Mac snatched an empty pop bottle from a case, sprinted to the crime scene (Winston still in lips) and let fly. The bottle caught the snarling menace flush in the forehead, dropping it in its tracks. The now-leaderless pack turned tail. Sandy was saved. Mac was our hero.

We learned decades later that Mac was a real hero. Like most World War II vets around Yorktown, "in the service" was all he'd say. In fact, Mac served as a fighter pilot—a profession with an exceedingly unfavorable actuarial table. His citation reads: "Marvin B. McElhiney (CSN: 0–25856), United States Marine Corps, awarded the Distinguished Flying Cross for extraordinary achievement while participating in aerial flight, in actions against enemy Japanese forces in the Pacific Theater of Operations during World War II."

CHAPTER 3

A Lawless Society

YORKTOWN WAS MOST NOTABLE for what it did not have.

Government remained so limited even Ron Paul would have approved. The town duly elected a mayor, Tom Whitney, a retiree in overalls. But Tom's powers were narrowly circumscribed. One of his most important roles was to address rabid dogs. When a canine foaming at the mouth appeared anywhere in town, Tom lifted his .22 rifle from its rack and strode to the scene like Wyatt Earp bound for the O.K. Corral. Young citizens watched in awe as Mayor Tom performed his legal duty.

No EPA or local equivalent deprived us of our natural right to smell burning leaves in autumn. Rather, voluminous leaf piles smoldered for hours. Household garbage—metal cans included—burned in backyards; no refuse pick-up service existed. Most sewage drained into septic tanks, which often leaked, requiring fragrant exhumation. Indeed, some sewage—as from Mac's slaughterhouse—simply flowed into surrounding cornfields.

There being no Yorktown police department, a Page County sheriff's deputy cruised town weekly. But he stopped only once that anyone could recall: to calm an Arkansas native who'd consumed too much Pabst Blue Ribbon in Clarinda. Law enforcement remained so limited because essentially no crime occurred. Keys routinely remained in the ignitions of parked cars. Folks could remember locking doors to their houses only during Charlie Starkweather's 1957–58 murder spree. (Starkweather, of Lincoln, Nebraska, was the Midwest's first modern serial killer.)

Government-mandated safety measures absented themselves from 1960s Yorktown, as from America generally. No seat belts in cars, much less airbags. Child car seats lay far in the future. The whole family hurtled unrestrained down the highway at 70 mph, ripe for a launching through the windshield that somehow never came. The notion of a bicycle helmet would have been laughable. A kid who lacked layers of elbow and knee scabs and an undiagnosed concussion or two by midsummer wasn't really trying.

Beyond fear itself, the only thing feared was Mrs. Yearous's ankle-biting geese. They formed a daunting gauntlet on the block-long walk to school.

CHAPTER 4

Endless Summer

CHILD MOLESTERS WERE ANOTHER horror alien to Yorktown. As a result, youngsters left home early every summer morning in search of adventure. Mothers were unconcerned for their whereabouts so long as a cow bell's clanging was answered for the mid-day meal. Confusion surrounded the proper name for this repast. Because local farmers consumed steaks, chops, and other heavy fare at noon, they referred to it as "dinner." Townsfolk, in turn, called it "lunch." "Dinner" having been pre-empted, farmers dubbed their evening meal "supper." We did too—meaning we ate breakfast, lunch, and supper. Never a dinner, except on Thanksgiving, Christmas, and Easter.

Lunch over, children resumed their wanderings around Yorktown and environs until the cow bell rang again for supper. Snake Creek was a favored spot for expeditions, water and mud being magnetic to the young. The crick was so murky no fish had ever been seen *in situ*. It was surmised, however, they must exist. No child owned an actual fishing pole, so string tied to handles of garden implements substituted. Safety pins served as hooks.

Against all odds, a fish—a scrawny bullhead—was landed. What now? A hole was dug and filled with water from a garden hose. Everyone expressed surprise when the trophy turned belly up only minutes later.

Trespass laws were on the books, but honored only in the breach. So long as a kid committed no affirmative mischief, why shouldn't he amble across an open field or rummage through an abandoned building? One such foray uncovered a cache of well-preserved movie posters, Tom Mix mainly. America's first movie cowboy, Mix made 336 movies between 1910 and 1935, all but nine silent. Another search uncovered an abandoned pack of Camel cigarettes. Coughing efforts to smoke them ensured none of us would grow up to fund the tobacco industry.

Once every summer or so, the children of Yorktown held an impromptu "dress-up parade." For some reason, many boys donned women's clothes; it would be called drag today. Prevailed upon to pull out the fire truck, Mac led the parade, siren blaring.

Buried treasure figured prominently in our summer thinking. A black iron disk stamped "Lucky Penny," the circumference of a coffee cup, emerged from a shallow grave in the front yard. This "penny" extolled virtues of the Denver Stockyards. Odd, as those yards were several hundred miles distant. Most Page County livestock met their maker much closer to home—in Omaha, Nebraska, or St. Joseph (always "St. Joe"), Missouri. Another summer we came into a silver dollar and buried our own treasure in the garden—precisely twenty paces due west of the third wooden fence post.

Hunting roadside ditches for other peoples' abandoned treasure—empty pop bottles—was a never-ending quest. Empties were redeemable at Mac's for the princely sum of two cents. It was beyond amazing that anyone would discard an item of such value, but they surely did. Meanwhile, future doctors and nurses anesthetized grasshoppers with rubbing alcohol and charted behavior as they regained consciousness.

Yorktown lacked sufficient children to field full sports teams. Baseball and football were three-on-three at best.

So we sought out other games. Andy-I-Over involved two teams alternately throwing a volley ball over a garage. Ball caught, the receiving side charged around the garage to blast a foe with it, thereby adding them to the receiving team. Hide and Seek was also popular, but troublesome, because the playing field was so vast. A hider could sprint to the far side of town, never to be found.

Who would "go first" was a constant issue in the summer games. It helped to have wise parents. In a favored method, one child picked a secret number between one and ten, and then two others selected their own numbers; closest to the secret number won. Our dad taught us always to let the other player pick first (which, favoring a personal lucky number, the player was only too happy to do). Then, unless the pick was five or six, Player B should select the number next in succession in the direction of five and six. For example: If Player A picked nine, Player B should pick eight, because Player A could win only if the secret number was nine or ten, making Player B's chances of victory 80 percent.

In addition to knowing probability theory, Dad was racially enlightened by local standards. He insisted that, in another popular method for selecting "go first"—Eeny, meeny, miny, moe—the subject caught by the toe be a "tiger."

The 1960s were a superb time to be a child not just in Yorktown. Every outdoor toy worth owning had been invented: the Frisbee, hula hoop, and skate board. Over a summer, a succession of fads was tried and abandoned: Super Balls (like a laser to nearest pane of glass), boomerangs (never came back), plastic airplanes propelled by a slingshot (smooth landing—on nearest roof).

"Clubs" were popular too. Rival sets of Yorktown children claimed separate clubhouses in the sand bins next to the abandoned rail line. Initiation rites involved the likes of scooping dog excrement with bare hands. Exclusionary rules applied. Some clubs were single-sex. Others had age requirements. But alliances shifted and rules with them. Sometimes a kid would pledge never to speak to fellow club members again. Usually this step was taken only following a firm invitation to join a rival club.

When all else failed in the pursuit of summer fun, we climbed the big elm to read books. The tree was surrounded by softball-size irises of every color combination, and the drone of locusts played a Southwest Iowa summer symphony.

CHAPTER 5

Town Tableau

BESIDES ITS MERCHANT CLASS (Mac and Mrs. Mac, the Eichhorsts), Yorktown housed a carpenter (another Eichhorst), a few farmers, many retirees, a teacher (our father), two preachers, folks who labored in Clarinda or Shenandoah, and even one who daily commuted the fifty miles to Omaha. Few women worked outside the home.

The unemployed consisted of a couple twenty-something men who spent their days sawing mounds of firewood, tinkering with motor vehicles to no perceptible effect, and silently walking town. They wore long-sleeved work shirts (top button always fastened) no matter how hot the weather. Truth be told, these mute wanderers would have been institutionalized in a more-metropolitan setting. But here they stayed a well-accepted part of the town tableau, cared for by their extended families.

Many houses in 1960s Yorktown were stocked with unfortunate blond furniture, heavy on the metal. This was Danish Modern disease, an indoor version of the Dutch Elm disease silently killing trees. Striving for modernity, one farm family razed its stately brick abode, replacing it with a wooden ranch house. They consigned all of the old house's dark-wood furniture to a bonfire, for it was not "modern." The sickness even infected Christmas, with modern metal trees taking the place of evergreens for a (blessedly short) time. These silver trees—Mac had one in his store window—changed color from orange, to pink, to blue, to yellow as an electronic wheel rotated nearby.

Despite location in one of the world's prime agricultural regions, typical Yorktown cuisine was, in a word, bland. Cooks utilized a short spice rack. Olive oil was unheard of; lard and Crisco ruled. Oleomargarine out-sold butter. Beef roasted until petrified, and vegetables boiled fervently to extinguish all nutrients. Potatoes shared the plate at essentially every meal.

Almost everyone in town tended a garden. The month of May meant radishes and lettuce; June brought strawberries; August, tomatoes and sweet corn. Even so, Yorktownians did their darnedest to avoid eating healthily. Fresh berries were heaped with white sugar, and tomato slices were coated with salt.

Only a generation or two removed from Europe, townspeople nonetheless drank pallid American beer and retained nothing of culinary value from the Old Country. Meal's end often featured canned fruit cocktail suspended in Jell-o of unnatural hues. Baked desserts—notably pies of fresh rhubarb and gooseberry—provided one oasis in the dessert desert.

The food rendered many women "pleasingly plump," in a term of the time. So they struggled into rubberized tubes of Lycra called girdles. Snaps on the girdle's bottom fringe held up brownish nylon stockings. Female eyeglasses swooped upward at their edges and often featured faux jewels. We called these "witch glasses"; how anyone ever found them attractive remains a mystery.

Clothing for men and children was ill-fitting and nondescript (the lime-green leisure suit was yet to come). Blue jeans chopped into "cutoffs" were a summertime uniform for kids; overalls were worn year-round by men. Many residents, particularly the elderly, did not waste cash on new-fangled deodorant, something humans had survived millennia without.

In addition to garden crops, Yorktown marked time with a succession of abundant flowers. First, crocuses peeked through lingering snow. Then daffodils, followed by tulips. For two weeks each spring, lilac bushes bloomed with an unforgettable fragrance that permeated town. Children learned a bedtime prayer: "Now I lay me down to sleep, I pray the Lord my soul to keep; if I should die before I wake, I pray the Lord my soul to take." Strange, as no child we knew had ever died in sleep, but the sentiment stuck. During June, we'd awake to balmy, flower-scented breezes and drowsily wonder: "Is this Heaven?" No, just Iowa.

St. Paul Lutheran School, Yorktown, Iowa

St. Paul Lutheran Church in 1995,
three years before it was destroyed by a suspicious fire

Richard B. Ulmer Sr., a city man proud of his cabbage

Tornado damage to Yorktown in 1964

The Ulmers in 1963

The Ulmer kids and tall corn

The Ulmer kids at the teacherage

The Main Street bandstand today

Yorktown scene, 2012

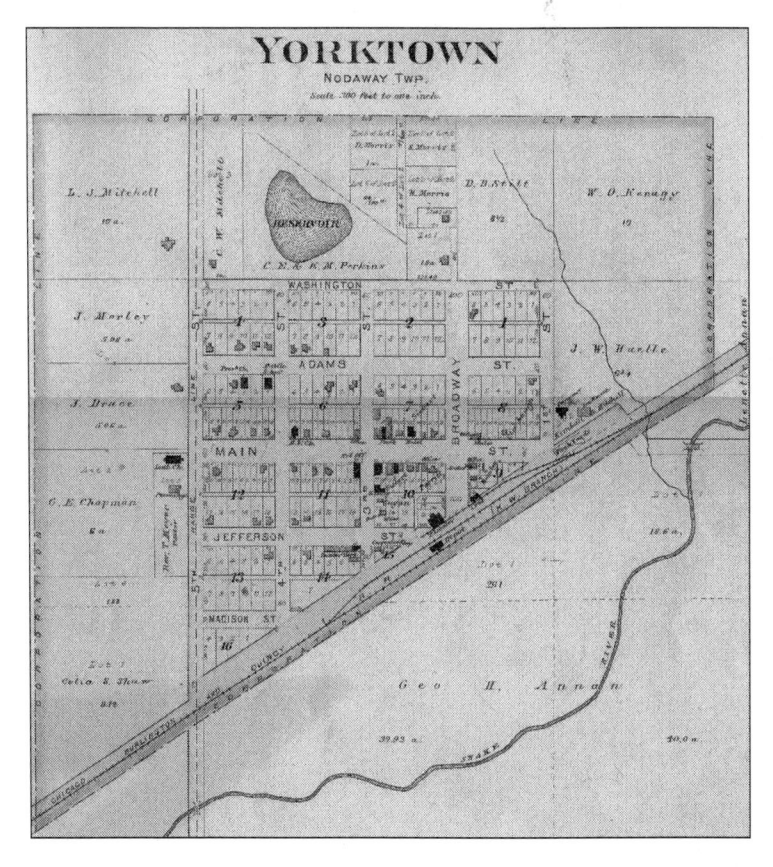

Yorktown plat map, 1902

CHAPTER 6

Monochrome

ANOTHER SIGNAL FEATURE of Yorktown was the utter absence of what the 21st century would call diversity. Everyone in town was Caucasian—always had been, always would be. We observed no black, Asian, or Latino/a person in Page County until the Kansas City Monarchs "colored" baseball club barnstormed Clarinda to drub the town team.

Likewise, though Iowa named itself after an Indian tribe—the Ioway people—no Native Americans were known to live in the county. English only was spoken.

More foreign language is heard in one trip down a California grocery aisle than was uttered in a Yorktown decade.

"Jew" was employed as a verb. At the same time, folks highly regarded the only Jewish person they actually knew, Clarinda's Dr. Frankel. His unorthodox methods including jabbing a child's teddy bear with his needle to demonstrate that a shot would not hurt.

Use of the "N" word was common, often directed at blacks in Omaha. For its spring play one year, the school put on a minstrel show. Students in blackface sang about "mammy's little babies" loving shortening bread. The next year, our dad brought in a black student teacher. After that, no minstrel shows. TV helped too. Cassius Clay (later Muhammad Ali) burst onto the black-and-white screen. He was colorful, brash, self-promoting, and a little loopy—so unlike a Yorktownian he might have been from another planet. We adored him. "Float like a butterfly, sting like a bee" appeared in many a school composition.

Yorktown was overwhelmingly Republican. A running joke had all the town's Democrats meeting around a single card table in Marrel Sump's living room. Local farmers called pestiferous gnats "Democrats." A straw poll at school showed Goldwater defeating Johnson soundly in the 1964 election—not exactly the national result. Mac, despite drawing a federal paycheck as postmaster, was wont to call LBJ "Old Squinty Eyes."

Homelessness was unknown, it being so cheap to live in Yorktown and so cold in winter the concept was infeasible. However, hoboes—a more-mobile prototype of the latter-day homeless—did occasionally filter through town while hitch-hiking Highway 2. Mom would have a hobo perform an odd job then feed him lunch. Why our house was Yorktown's hobo stop was revealed when we re-painted the front fence and found a strange symbol drawn in a secluded spot. This was the hobo way of communicating "food available here" to others who would follow.

No one talked much about it, but diversity of a sort existed in Yorktown. It was religious in nature. We Lutherans attended a red brick church on the south side of Main Street, while the Methodists had a smaller white wooden one on the street's north side. All the Lutherans were German. Methodists were a more ethnically mixed lot, but still all Northern European.

With notable exceptions, Methodists trended lower on the socio-economic scale. They were the kind of folk who possessed four derelict Chevys as a boneyard of parts to keep one vehicle of the same model operational. Some Methodist houses still lacked indoor plumbing. However, the notion that Sears catalogs were utilized in outhouses was a rural legend.

The Lutherans were convinced the Methodists were hell-bound when they newly employed a *female* pastor.

Soon thereafter, mischief arose in the countryside. Farmers who kept tanks of gasoline in their fields to fuel tractors began to find the tanks drained. It happened repeatedly. Then late one night, Mrs. Methodist Pastor's teenage son was found on a country road next to his stalled '54 Ford, its engine smoking. A farmer had filled his field tank with high-test aviation fuel rather than gasoline. I-told-you-so's volleyed across Main Street.

CHAPTER 7

Mass Communicating

COMMUNICATION WAS A-CHANGIN' after mid-century in Yorktown.

When we hit town in 1957, telephony was still Wilma Chapman. Wilma lived her entire long life in a small house on the west end of Main Street across from the Lutheran parsonage. Yorktown's telephone switchboard—"the board"—dominated her parlor.

The telephonic device in each home was a wall-mounted rectangular wooden box. One turned a crank to summon operator Wilma to her board. She then plugged in cords to place the call. Speech was through a black metal snout. You listened via a separate black earpiece hanging hooked to the wooden box's side.

Because she could listen in on calls, Wilma had her fingers not just on phone cords, but on the pulse of Yorktown life. Our family's introduction to Wilma came when we were considering moving to town and phoned for the Lutheran pastor. Leaning out her window, Wilma observed, "I don't see his car in the driveway right now; you'll have to call back."

Telephone wires were expensive to string and maintain, so customers had "party lines" that shared a loop of wire with a few other homes. Each party had a specified number of rings to signal an incoming call. It was no party to share such a line with a loquacious teenager. But there was a 1960s app for that: You listened to her calls clandestinely (taking care not to breathe too loudly) and then spread intimate details of her relationships.

In an emergency such as a fire, Wilma could ring everyone at once. Similar to a group e-mail, only louder. An era ended on December 21, 1960, when the Clarinda phone company took over with rotary-dial phones. The Yorktown board fell silent.

Television came less abruptly, with gradual market penetration. For those who had sets, only three commercial channels were on offer: CBS, NBC, and ABC. No channel-surfing then; a knob had to be twisted by hand (after a scrum with siblings to settle what show to view). The so-called "Fairness Doctrine" required minute-for-minute rebuttal of any political opinion, so the somnolent Eric Sevareid passed for news commentary. Prime-time programming consisted of wall-to-wall Westerns, with a few variety shows in the brief pauses between fisticuffs and gun play.

Mac received the town's daily mail in a faded white canvas bag from Clarinda, then sorted it into the individual boxes noted earlier. Retired men gathered around a hot stove waiting for Mac to finish. Those who believed TV must culturally edify the populace would have been sorely disappointed by these proceedings. Much talk was of "All-Star Wrestling" seen on Omaha TV the night before. The long-reigning champ was Verne Gagne, a former collegiate grappler who was balding and rather dumpy even by the pre-steroid standards of the day. Nonetheless, Verne prevailed against a cast of villainous characters twice his size. The men of Yorktown closely analyzed every televised match, actually seeming to believe results were not preordained.

It was a golden age of local radio. Shenandoah stations dominated the region. KMA was the voice of the Earl May Seed Company. Rival Henry Field Seed Company owned KFNF ("First in News"). For rural listeners (live)stock prices and weather were top-of-mind. Reports from the yards in Omaha and St. Joe had a lexicon all their own. "Barrows and gilts" were young castrated male and young female hogs, respectively. "Cutters and canners" were low-end cattle.

Radio hosts like Frank Field (on KMA despite Field family membership) issued frequent weather forecasts. Today's sophisticated computer models were unavailable, so Frank consulted indicators like clothes drying on a line outside his studio window. Predictably, his prognostications were wrong more often than not.

For women, the shows from Shenandoah provided recipes and cleaning tips. It was the event of the Yorktown season when radio homemaker Martha Bohlsen once visited to display her slides from a vacation to Denmark.

Newspapers remained largely unchanged during this epoch. Southwest Iowa was a circulation battleground among the *Omaha World-Herald* (closest city), *Des Moines Register* (state capital), and *Council Bluffs Nonpareil* (Omaha's twin city across the Missouri River). Only the *Nonpareil* offered daily home delivery in Yorktown—by your writer. The other two papers were available on Sunday. The dark cloud on newspapers' horizon—the Internet—was still barely forming in Al Gore's brain.

CHAPTER 8

Outside Lands

EVEN WITH MASS MEDIA, the outside world intruded on Yorktown life only rarely. The Cuban missile crisis of October 1962 certainly did. America and the Soviet Union were poised to nuke each other into oblivion. Even small children knew it. But there were no duck-and-cover drills in Yorktown like those from grainy TV footage of the time. We sat less than fifty miles from Strategic Air Command headquarters south of Omaha, a prime Soviet target. Instantaneous vaporization assumed, no one bothered with protective measures.

President Kennedy's assassination on November 22, 1963, was another dark day. History tells of school children cheering the news in right-leaning regions of the country. Not Yorktown. The Chicago machine may well have stolen the 1960 election for him, but JFK was nonetheless our president.

Most of the time, our outside world was Clarinda. At 9 A.M. every Saturday without fail, the family piled into the car to drive six miles east down Highway 2. Everyone else in Yorktown did the same, though the more adventurous chose Saturday evening. This was called "going to town." Yorktown might rightfully have argued that it too was a town, so we were already in one. But man could not live by Mac's and Eichhorsts' alone. More stores were required.

Clarinda had a classic Midwestern town square surrounding a classic county courthouse with classic marble staircases. It was all right out of a Grant Wood painting. On the courthouse's lush lawn stood the obligatory monument to Union soldiers. Though it bordered Missouri, Page County's Civil War sympathies lay firmly to the North. Incongruously, Santa Claus maintained a red hut next to the war monument where he appeared on December Saturdays.

Walmart had yet to obliterate small-town commerce, so a circuit of the square was always in order. One might start on the south side at F.W. Woolworth (roasted peanuts, soda fountain) and then stride over to

J.C. Penney on the west. These names are still with us, but the Clarinda versions were much cozier, had wooden floors, and smelled like proper stores (simultaneously musty and new) in a way the modern mall never does.

Occasionally we acquired a new pair of shoes at the Poll Parrot store; they came with a plastic whistle. A Green Stamp store also graced the square. The stamps were awarded with purchases at local merchants. One glued these into "books" with pages the size of personal checks, and then, after a mountain of books was amassed, redeemed them for a cherished item like a softball glove. The barber shop provided Dad's fortnightly 75-cent crew cut, then it was off to Hy-Vee for the week's groceries. Annually we visited the dentist, just off the Clarinda square, for checkups. Results never varied: no fluoride, no flossing, no teeth-cleaning, but no cavities.

The public library was our penultimate stop (less opportunity that way to lose books before returning to Yorktown). A building almost as grand as the courthouse, the library had been gifted to Clarinda (long before that became a verb) by steel magnate Andrew Carnegie. A total of 1,689 "Carnegie libraries" were magnanimously spread across the United States.

A downstairs children's section had its own librarian. A six-book weekly maximum applied; for us it was also a mandatory minimum. Even then, we quickly exhausted supply and were reduced to reading biographies of lesser lights like Light Horse Harry Lee. Upstairs had the "adult books" (this was before pornography became "adult"). An impressive foot-high cast iron statute of Lincoln and his Cabinet memorialized the "Team of Rivals" of Doris Kearns Goodwin's great book-to-come.

We once selected a thin volume excoriating evils of capitalism in the auto industry. It was excised from the library after Dad deemed it a "communist book." He later lodged a similar complaint about the "Merry Xmas" sign on the phone-company building across from the library. But Dad missed the mark that time, for X is the first letter in the Greek word for Christ.

Few trips to town ended without a final stop, at the filling station. During "gas wars," prices dropped into the teens of cents per gallon. Even then, a friendly attendant filled the tank and washed the car windows. When gas stations weren't competing quite so fiercely on price, motorists received a free drinking glass or eating utensil with each fill-up.

CHAPTER 9

Black Gold

YORKTOWN IS SURROUNDED BY some of the world's richest farm land. Dark-chocolate in color, it is dirt California gardeners would gladly pay $9.99 a twenty-pound bag for. Yet from Yorktown this fertile soil stretches millions of acres in every direction.

The entire system was set up in squares back in the 1800s. Square counties march in tiers across Iowa from east to west. Within counties are six-mile-square "townships." Within each township lie thirty-six one-mile-square "sections" of precisely 640 acres. Superintending all this geometry was the farmer—call him a "grower," as in California, and he'd look at you quizzically.

The 1960s Yorktown-area farmer came in a variety of shapes and sizes, but four common characteristics distinguished him from the general populace. The first was his "farmer's tan," particularly in summer. He wore a baseball-style logo cap provided gratis by the brand of seed corn he planted. Below the seed-cap line, his face was beet-red. Above the line, his dome (for an inordinate amount of farmers were bald or balding) was ghostly white. Thus, gazing out over a church congregation of farmers was like viewing a range of snowy peaks.

The farmer's second signal feature was his hands. When all fingers remained fully present (given farm accidents, this was not always so), they were massive, gnarled, and powerful from years of outdoor work. The farmer usually proffered a dish-rag handshake, so as not to mangle the recipient. But woe to any limp-wristed city fella who offended the farmer and received a full-force grip.

Third, the adjectives "taciturn" and "stoic" were coined with him in mind. If he was golfing—a surprising number of farmers were duffers—and hit a hole-in-one, he would calmly retrieve his ball and remark on the weather. Questions were usually answered monosyllabically, "yep" and "nope" predominating. Some attributed the farmer's nature to years alone in the fields. Others, to a life in which one timely rain could turn a year.

Finally, the Southwest Iowa farmer was almost universally good of heart. A farmer hospitalized at harvest time would return home to find his crops in the barn. Unbidden, neighbors had pitched in, simply because it was the right thing to do. A motorist stuck in snow or mud could always walk to the nearest farm house to be freed by a tractor. An attempt at payment would be rejected with a silent wave of the farmer's hand.

The typical Page County farm raised a limited menu of crops and livestock, but in prodigious quantities. Corn was king. Iowa still annually produces more than any other state: about 2.5 billion bushels on 14 million acres. This is not the "sweet corn" of corn-on-the-cob. (Iowa farmers commercially grow less than 5,000 acres of that.) Rather, it is "field corn," with hard kernels. Soybeans (mispronounced "soy-ee" beans in Page County) ranked second, followed by alfalfa grown as hay.

Cattle were mainly raised for meat rather than milk, this being Iowa and not Wisconsin. The reddish-brown-and-white models were Herefords; the black, Angus. In the 1960s, more farmers began to fatten cattle on corn in "feedlots" instead of on pasture grass. And "fat" was the appropriate word. Steaks of the day—before diet police—were richly marbled, like those in today's Argentina and Brazil.

Many motorists held their noses when driving past the aromatic feedlots. In contrast, the farmer took a deep whiff, smiled, and mused, "Smells like money in the bank." Pigs too were popular in Page County. Only a few oddballs raised sheep or goats. Chickens were the farm wife's responsibility.

The farmer and his family resided in a house surrounded by barns and out buildings. This was "the place," as in "the Lester Nothwehr place." Structures were rarely painted because winter was too cold for that and the year was otherwise spent farming. Happily this neglect yielded weathered barn wood for city folks' rec rooms. The 1960s brought the A.O. Smith Harvestore, a massive cylinder for storing grain. From far above, these appear as dark blue dots on a farmstead. While in the air, a ready way to discern that one's jet is *not* over Southwest Iowa are large circles in the farm fields. These evidence center-pivot irrigation and don't begin until the Great Plains in mid-Nebraska, where precipitation is less abundant and reliable.

Sports had yet to become a national mania by the '60s. Only baseball had many fans and, though Kansas City was the closest major league city, Page County followed a mix of St. Louis Cardinals, Minnesota Twins, and Chicago Cubs or White Sox. Instead of a sports team, a farmer's primary allegiance was to his machinery. His pickup truck was a Ford, Chevy, or Dodge, in that order. Switching brands was as rare as divorcing a wife. Likewise with tractors. It was John Deere, Massey Ferguson, Case, or Farmall—for life. Tractor-pulling at the county fair in Clarinda featured flame-belching behemoths towing concrete sleds (a feat no tractor ever performed on the farm) for brand-name bragging rights.

Rural life in America tends to be homogenized by those who have never lived it. Many, for example, harbor the misconception that Midwestern farmers raise vegetables and fruit for market. But the growing season is too short, so a Southwest Iowa farm family gets its produce from California or a can, just like everyone else.

Also contrary to expectations, few Yorktown farm families of the 1960s favored country western music. KMA played the likes of Nat King Cole and Ray Charles. Kids preferred rock & roll. Likewise, only one family around Yorktown—aptly surnamed Rope—wore cowboy garb or followed rodeo.

CHAPTER 10

Lesser Creatures

THE VIEWS OF YORKTOWN and today's urbanite diverge perhaps most starkly on the subject of animal life. Few Yorktown farmers or townspeople would have gratuitously harmed a lesser creature. At the same time, there was no PETA-style anthropomorphizing. God created animals to benefit mankind—it said so right in Genesis 1.

Pets abounded in Yorktown. One widow went so far as to live with chickens in her house. (No, they were not potty-trained.) On the farm, the concern was often too many pets. The farm-cat population in particular had a way of spiraling out of control. But no one saw the need for a spay-and-neuter clinic. Simply backing the family car from the garage into a crowd of cats yielded a series of crunches that tended to resolve the Malthusian predicament.

Sentiment never stood in the way of livelihood. On one farm, a beloved dog—call him Rover—committed the mortal offense of killing chickens. While younger family members were told he'd "run away," Rover actually wound up behind the barn on the wrong end of the farmer's .22.

Livestock were similarly perceived. The 4-H calf, an honored tradition in Iowa, was incessantly washed, curried, and otherwise pampered for the big day at the county fair. Then later, blue ribbon or no, off to slaughter.

Yorktown children were introduced early to this circle of life and death. Even when we were as young as four or five, Mac allowed us to take in the proceedings at his slaughterhouse. A bullet between the eyes, a tumble inside through a trap door, throat slit, then evisceration and vigorous sawing. Finally, another hide added to a salted stack and, if the deceased was a pig, a tasty vat of chitterlings (a.k.a. "chittlins"—boiled small intestines). No better preparation could be had for anatomy class or life in the emergency room or on the police beat.

Observing animal slaughter served in other ways as well. Take the expression "running around like a chicken with its head cut off." It is, we learned, an apt metaphor. One Thanksgiving our neighbors, the Berringers, publically put hatchet to a turkey in their backyard and the beheaded bird chased Ulmer sisters for fully thirty seconds before collapsing.

When time came to stock freezers with chickens, farm wives had differing methods of dispatch. Some simply wrung the bird's neck. Others forced the head between two nails on a board and chopped. Pulling feathers from chicken carcasses defined labor-intensity. Then the edible innards—heart, liver, gizzard—were excavated. The latter held greatest allure, as diamond rings were said to have been discovered inside them.

While domesticated animal life was plentiful in the Yorktown vicinity, wildlife was not, contrary to the myth of country hills teeming with game. Maybe it was lack of wooded areas; every inch of arable land having been put to crop production. Perhaps abundance of potent pesticides and herbicides played a role. In any event, we never sighted a deer near a deer-crossing sign, or anywhere else for that matter.

CHAPTER 11

As You Sow

People of Southwest Iowa were, as a rule, long-lived. Many achieved the biblical four score and ten. This was not due to any special diet or exercise regimen. Daily life itself was exercise, and meat and potatoes served just fine, thank you.

On the other hand, life could end quickly and brutally. Tractors of the 1960s were not yet equipped with roll bars. Many lives were snuffed out too young. Most farmers had narrowly avoided being pulled into machinery. A man struck a match when the pilot light flickered out in his hog shed and was blown to kingdom come. Periodically a fellow would fall into a large bin of shelled corn to be suffocated. If someone tried to help, he too might be sucked under.

Farmers around Yorktown viewed themselves as rugged individualists, and rightly so. They were sole proprietors who annually put much, if not all, of their capital at risk. Most were intelligent, but farm life often perplexed.

The 1960s farmer produced unprecedented yields, more than enough to feed America. Yet people in the Third World were said to be (in fact, were) starving. Then why was the federal government paying him *not* to grow crops—to keep land idle?

Likewise, the more successful the farmer became at producing, the lower commodity prices seemed to fall. A union of sorts formed: the National Farmers Organization. It withheld products from market—even poured fresh milk onto the ground. That waste of God's gifts did not sit well with German-Lutheran farm folk.

The farmer cared little for Big Government, particularly LBJ's Great Society with its welfare payments to people who did not (some said would not) work. Yet the 4-H Club ("Head, Heart, Hands, and Health") his children enjoyed was itself a federal program. Another club for farm youth, Future Farmers of America, wasn't government-sponsored. But the FFA consumed too much time—hence the sobriquet "Father Farms Alone."

Daylight Savings Time was the Devil's doing. Some farmers refused to reset their watches. The objection was that DST enabled city folk to golf after work but kept farmers in the field longer. They did not want to hear this was illogical, as hours of daylight remained precisely the same with or without "savings."

In 50-year retrospect, 1960s Southwest Iowa experienced a green revolution. Farming improved on every front. Hills were terraced to avoid runoff of valuable rain water and soil. Crops rotated over time—soybeans replenished nitrogen in soil for corn. Superior herbicides and pesticides were formulated. Hybridization of crop varieties boosted production by many bushels per acre.

Bigger and better farm equipment appeared. Before, it took several men to bale hay. One drove the tractor; others picked up and stacked bales on a wagon. Working on such a baling crew—including drinking from the communal water jug immediately after a tobacco-chewer—was a rural youngster's rite of passage. After innovation, one man could bale hay alone. He hoisted huge circular bales with a large lance on the front of a tractor.

Not only were fewer hands required to farm identical amounts of land, but more land was needed to carry investment in the bigger-and-better machinery. Farms had to get larger, which again meant fewer farmers. Hired hands—an important source of employment for less-gifted males—became ever rarer. Most sons and daughters could not stay on the farm. The math was irresistible.

A successful way of life thus sowed seeds of its own decline. Every town in Page County lost population between 1960 and 2010. Many schools, churches, and businesses withered on the vine.

CHAPTER 12

Out of Hannover

OUR AMERICAN MELTING POT holds, by far, more people of German ethnicity than any other. Today, more than 50 million Americans—17 percent of the population—report German ancestry. Few people know this because two world wars taught German-Americans a low profile was preferable to being interned like the Japanese.

America attracted Germans with its ready availability of prime farm land. Many German Lutherans also disliked a state church that tilted liberal. The story of

Yorktown (indeed, of the entire lower Midwest) is in large part the story of these folk—people with no-doubt German names like Nothwehr, Behrhorst, Wellhausen, Eichhorst, Windhorst, Gerdts, Muller, and Huseman.

In 1895, the Yorktown Lutherans named their church St. Paul's (the possessive later fell away). This commemorated Dr. Martin Luther's favorite author. The congregation soon joined the Lutheran Church-Missouri Synod ("LCMS" for short). Synod means "walking together," which is odd, as the denomination has been schismatic from inception. Its first leader, accused of financial corruption and sexual immorality, was introduced to the Mississippi River in a rowboat, on the Missouri side, and ordered to paddle across to Illinois, never to return.

Like those at most LCMS churches, early Yorktown Lutherans spoke German in their church and elementary school. (In a quaint artifact of that time, the LCMS still retains an "English District" of the churches across America that declined Deutsch from the start.) In World War I's aftermath, a Yorktown mob threatened to lynch St. Paul's Pastor Horn. The mob demanded, and got, an immediate switch to full-time English at St. Paul School.

By 1960, a few old-timers could stumble through "O Tannenbaum" and "Stille Nacht" at Christmas, but little other Old County influence remained. Indeed, already at that time, most Yorktown Lutherans could not say where in Germany their roots were planted. Google their distinctive surnames and many vectors point to the Hannover region of Lower Saxony, but they did not immigrate to America in a group like many German Lutherans did.

Detachment from Germany made these folks no less a community. St. Paul was their center of life. The church social was prime time for "fellowship." Congregants gathered in the church hall at night for some perfunctory reason, but a social's real object was food, and plenty of it. Potluck dishes spread across groaning tables. Casseroles topped with potato-chip crumbs or hard-boiled egg slices were legion. In summer, ice cream was freshly churned. All was washed down with "church coffee," a faintly brown brew that had experienced only the briefest exposure to any grounds.

A "Ladies Aid" club kept most of the isolated farm wives sane compiling church cookbooks and the like. "Walther League" was the club for teenagers. It was named after LCMS Leader #2, who'd shoved Leader #1's rowboat into the Mississippi.

A striking amount of St. Paul's social life revolved around the institution of marriage. Wedding planners anticipated 90 percent attendance by invitees (compared to 50 to 60 percent expected in the city). The wedding, often a quite liquid affair, was first. Following in a few weeks was a "shivaree," in which the newlyweds' home was surrounded at night by members of a young-marrieds club (the "Merry Matrimonials") rudely banging on pots and pans. This folk custom's purpose was unclear; it certainly disrupted procreational activity. Later, a church banquet celebrated the 25th anniversary. Then, Lord willing, the 50th. A surprising number of couples even recorded seventy-five anniversaries. Divorce being all but unheard of, and the church having 300 members, these celebrations filled calendars.

Music was a Dr. Luther forte and his church steeped in it. Every child in a Lutheran grade school was trained to read music, and choir was mandatory. This led to St. Paul sights like an expensive twelve-rank pipe organ, seemingly out of place in a small-town church. A men's chorus of fifteen farmers and laborers turned out high-quality hymns in four-part harmony.

Christmas and Easter were high holidays. The Christmas Eve pageant was a staple. Unfairly, Poor-Johnny-(and Jane)-One-Notes got the prized roles—Mary, Joseph, shepherds, angels, wise men. This was because "dressed parts" were not called upon to sing. In another Lutheran country tradition, when the Christmas Eve service ended the church rewarded each child with a brown paper bag of nuts, chocolate clusters, and an orange. This elicited even more excitement than poring over the Sears Christmas catalog for the preceding weeks.

Yorktown

At Easter, girls wore frilly pastel dresses (for younger siblings it might be the year's only new garment) and patent leather shoes. An Easter "sunrise service" was often scheduled lakeside at Pioneer Park on Highway 2. Inevitably snow or rain cancelled it.

Tithing—contributing 10 percent of family income (gross or net of taxes was never quite clear)—was widely practiced at St. Paul. Perhaps it remained so due to the enforcement mechanism: a report of every family's annual giving, to the penny, in a booklet published to the entire church membership.

CHAPTER 13

The Call

FOR DECADES, IOWA CAUCUSES have kicked off presidential primary season. Every four years, the national news media tut-tuts about teetotaler Iowa "evangelicals" bloc-voting as instructed by their fanatical pastors at religious revivals. As so often happens when it deigns to alight in a flyover state, the media gets this almost entirely wrong.

A large share of "evangelicals" in Iowa are Lutherans like those around Yorktown. But no Missouri Synod pastor would countenance endorsing a politician. "Render to Caesar the things that are Caesar's and to God the things that are God's," he would quote. Teetotaling? Why, Jesus's first miracle changed water into vintage wine, and Luther himself was nothing if not religious about his beer-drinking. Moreover, emotionalism breeds Jimmy Swaggarts—the polar opposite of a stolid LCMS pastor.

The "divine Lutheran service" as practiced at St. Paul-Yorktown in the 1960s began with the public confession of "a poor, miserable sinner"—the church-goer. Segue to a rote liturgy sprinkled with Latin titles only the pastor could translate (but never did). Then a sermon structured on the tried-and-true dichotomy of Law and Gospel. All this was served with heavy dollops of Luther's writings—so heavy, in fact, that the Holy Trinity almost became a quartet.

The "general prayer" followed. Every ailing parishioner and her malady got a shout-out twice—once before prayer, when the ailing were lengthily listed, and then again when each was lengthily prayed for. Holy Communion was also serious business. When congregants left church early, one St. Paul pastor sprinted outside—black robe flowing in the breeze—with the bread and wine.

Evangelism, called "missions," focused on red, yellow, and brown people overseas. "Here am I, send me! Send me!" Yorktown Lutherans fervently sang. This had no application to a non-German one might actually meet in the Yorktown community; they were most likely Methodists anyway. As a result, St. Paul's new members were progeny of the old.

If this all (save the Luther bit) sounds vaguely Catholic, it was. But that's the last thing a 1960s Lutheran pastor wanted to hear. He spent much of his time pondering whether Catholics were ticketed for heaven or not.

The "divine call" is another unique aspect of Missouri-Synod Lutheranism. No bishops exist to assign pastors or teachers to local congregations, so another mechanism is required. A congregation "issues" a "call" to a pastor or teacher educated at an LCMS seminary or college. The Holy Spirit then determines whether the candidate "accepts" or "returns" the call.

The potential for LCMS congregations to use the call process to raid one another's staff is readily apparent. Just that occurred in 1959 when St. Paul's Pastor Schroeder was called by a congregation in Nebraska. The burghers of St. Paul—who, truth told, had a well-deserved reputation for parsimony—decided to assist the Spirit by topping up Pastor Schroeder's existing salary. However, "after prayerful consideration," he nonetheless opted for the new position (with its still-higher remuneration).

The Lutheran call is more than an eccentricity. In 2012, it determined what the *New York Times* termed the

U.S. Supreme Court's "most significant religious liberty decision in two decades." An LCMS church in Michigan, Hosanna-Tabor, fired a teacher from its school after she sued over an employment dispute rather than settle out of court. The Supreme Court ruled that, because the teacher was "called," she was a minister of the church, and it thus had a First Amendment right to discharge her notwithstanding state employment law. The decision: Lutherans, 9; Forces of Evil, 0.

CHAPTER 14

All Above Average

HOMESPUN HUMORIST Garrison Keillor often tweaks a Minnesota town where "all the children are above average," but that is not far from truth. For decades, students in Iowa and its neighboring states have topped national rankings on achievement tests. On average, they really are above average. This has engendered a long-flowing brain drain little noted on the coasts. The Midwest sends a never-ending stream of engineers, doctors, lawyers, and business people to California, New York, and Texas.

Education in Iowa is successful because it is highly valued. Schools are edifices, commonly the most ornate and substantial structures in town. Even in wealthy California school districts, buildings are comparative hovels—flimsy single-story stucco that could not withstand a sustained Iowa wind.

So it was in 1960s Yorktown. Public-school kids were bussed into Clarinda, the Yorktown public school having been converted to a county center for what the time called "retarded" students. Thus, "the school" in town was St. Paul Lutheran, owned and operated by the church of the same name, and superintended from 1957 to 1966 by our dad.

St. Paul was one of nearly 1,000 Missouri Synod grade schools in America. Long the nation's second-largest private school system after the Catholics, it rested on Synod's excellent set of teachers colleges, all named Concordia.

In the World War I era, Nebraska's attempt to ban German from Lutheran schools led to the U.S. Supreme Court decision *Meyer v. Nebraska* (the Lutherans won that one too). *Meyer* in turn provided precedent for the Supreme Court's 1973 landmark abortion decision, *Roe v. Wade*. On a more notorious note, Kennedy assassin Lee Harvey Oswald attended a Lutheran school in the Bronx, albeit briefly.

A recent U.S. Department of Education study found that, controlling for students' family income and ethnicity, private schools do not, in fact, greatly outperform public schools. One exception: Lutheran schools, which the Education Department credited with the nation's best academic achievement. The general public knows none of this due to strict application of a core Lutheran teaching: "Don't get a big head."

St. Paul Lutheran School of Yorktown was a trim, red-brick building constructed in 1949—the date on the Lincoln penny pressed into its flagpole's concrete base. A brief flight of steps led up to two classrooms. These were the "Lower Room" (grades K-4) and the "Upper Room" (grades 5–8), though both were on the same story. A third room sandwiched between held a few library books, meager science apparatus, and a jar filled with sand dollars. These were a wonder, for many people in Yorktown lived complete lives without seeing an ocean in person—the nearest being 1,000 miles away.

In the late 1950s, the school transitioned from rows of desks on wooden rails to the modern freestanding kind. Eliminated were desk inkwells where girls' pigtails were dipped in days before ballpoint pens.

St. Paul was built into the side of a hill, allowing for a basement gymnasium. The basketball court was not quite regulation size—high-arching shots scraped the ceiling—and was closely surrounded by wall-mounted benches that opened many head gashes.

No one considered the legal consequences of playground equipment either. A squeaky swing set sent riders fifteen feet into the atmosphere. Rumor had it that one St. Paul student actually flew "over the top" on his swing, to complete a 360-degree circuit. A merry-go-round scraped many a dizzy knee.

Another diabolical device—long since removed from most playgrounds by the liability-conscious—was the teeter-totter. This was a lengthy wooden plank fixed at midpoint over a raised iron bar. The rider on one side rose five feet in the air, while the other went to ground, then vice versa. Eventually the down-position rider gleefully bailed out, sending his opposite number plummeting painfully to earth.

No government program provided school lunch, though a Clarinda dairy delivered individual-size bottles of chocolate milk. Metal lunch boxes with matching thermos bottles mainly featured themes from westerns and other TV shows.

In the Lower Room, watching Wayne Goecker extricate his hotdog provided daily lunchtime drama. Wayne's mom would partially cook a dog, then tie a string around it, and insert it into a hot-water thermos bottle. That a hotdog expands as it takes on water apparently was unaccounted for. Some days, Wayne pulled the string gently—dog broke, to jeers of classmates. Other days, he gave a swift tug—same result. He even tried coaxing the dog out by talking to it—to no avail. It's a wonder Wayne wasn't scarred for life by this daily Yorktown drama. But for years he happily operated an auto repair garage in Yorktown.

CHAPTER 15

Two-Room School

In the 1960s, St. Paul's Lower Room was taught by a succession of young graduates of the Concordia teachers college in Seward, Nebraska: Miss Krenz (severe "witch glasses"), Miss Ficken (red gingham dress), and Miss Jedlicka (broke pure-German mold by hailing from a Bohemian sector of the Cornhusker State). When "Miss" became "Mrs." ("Ms." did not yet exist), the Lower Room teacher "retired." She might rejoin the Lutheran workforce after her children had grown.

Our dad, meanwhile, was school principal and taught the Upper Room. Also serving as school janitor, he was mightily enthused when chemically treated dry mops were introduced in the early 1960s. Had Dad licensed his "look"—Buddy Holly glasses, short-sleeved white shirt, tie, plastic pocket protector—he'd have reaped millions from Silicon Valley engineers of succeeding decades.

How could a classroom teacher possibly educate twenty-plus children in four different grades? Actually, a two-room school had its advantages. A high-achieving second-grader might vault ahead to third- or fourth-grade material. Working on one's own without constant guidance from a teacher bred self-reliance. And classroom din was excellent preparation for the open-floor work spaces prevalent in business today.

Reading was taught by phonics; the student was to "s-ou-nd ou-t" each word. Spelling words were memorized; no one knew computerized spell-checking waited around the corner. The latest "new math" was taught until supplanted by the new new math. The curriculum contained no sex education. Daily observers of animal life, farm children had no need of it. A Hereford bull just south of the Lower Room softball field demonstrated for non-farm Yorktown kids.

Mr. Ulmer—even we, his children, called him that at school—was a talented teacher. He constantly questioned students, pitting one's views against another's to test and refine. We didn't know then, but this was the Socratic method used in law school. Mr. Ulmer was also famed for requiring a 200-word composition every week. A picture from a magazine or a brief title—say, "Something Big"—was posted as the subject matter. Students prepared for public speaking by reading best efforts aloud in class.

Religion class focused on Luther's Small Catechism, in which the Great Reformer would set down a teaching, followed by the mantra: "This is most certainly true." For some reason, all Old Testament kings of Israel and Judah were memorized in order of succession, including whether each was "bad" (all of Israel's kings and most of Judah's) or "good."

After Thanksgiving, the school's street-facing windows were painted with Christmas cheer and titles of carols in varying scripts. At night, interior lights remained burning to illuminate the festive scenes. It was a fantastic show for the two or three cars passing each evening.

Sports were emphasized. St. Paul's fierce (indeed, only) rival in athletics was Immanuel, a Lutheran school northwest of Clarinda. Presaging Crips and Bloods, Immanuel's color was blue and St. Paul's red. Students at both schools were what baseball people call "country strong" from work on the farm.

Each school had many talented athletes, but Immanuel's most storied was Frank Sunderman; St.

Paul's, Dennis Behrhorst. Both went on to college football—Frank as quarterback for the Iowa Hawkeyes, and Denny as a flanker and defensive back for the Drake Bulldogs. Thus, two tiny Lutheran schools in a corner of Iowa produced more Division I football players in a year than does the entire San Francisco public school system. Denny's feats were legendary. He could dunk a basketball as a sixth-grader, and he single-handedly ended flag football as an inter-school sport by eschewing flags and pulverizing an Immanuel ball carrier.

It is said the state of Nebraska has but two sports: football and spring football. Across the Missouri River in Iowa, athletics were more varied, but the schedule remained as constant as the seasons. Fall meant touch football at lunchtime and recess, but also softball. Winter featured two basketball games against Immanuel at a neutral gym in Clarinda. Spring brought home-and-away matchups in softball, complete with iced tubs of orange, strawberry, and grape Nesbitt's pop.

Field Day capped the spring sports calendar. Competition included normal track-and-field fare—the high jump often ended prematurely when the bamboo crossbar shattered—but also non-Olympic events like the three-legged race, shoe kick, and softball throw. Tug-of-wars were abandoned due to risk of injury (and because Immanuel so often prevailed). Field Day awards were blue, red, or white ribbons snipped with scissors and stapled to index cards with the event's name typed.

Though this preceded Title IX, small-town Iowa was ahead of its time. St. Paul girls competed in all sports save football—sometimes with the boys, but often on their own teams that faced off with Immanuel. Indeed, Iowa was nationally known for a girls' high school basketball tournament that drew more statewide attention than the male version.

The sexes also played together at recess. A brutal game called Battle Ball left angry welts on girls' legs, as they wore skirts. Miss Krenz mounted a campaign to ban Battle Ball, but Yorktown culture won out. Recess ended with the boys retreating to the single toilet in a dingy restroom and filling it from every direction simultaneously. This was considered up-to-date; Immanuel still used an outhouse.

The social calendar was filled with non-sports events as well: roller-skating parties, school plays, and the end-of-year picnic. One day during fall semester, a farm father would arrive after school on a tractor, pulling a wagon lined with hay bales. Students climbed aboard for a hayrack ride through the countryside. Later in the evening, hotdogs and marshmallows incinerated on sticks over a bonfire.

CHAPTER 16

Ulmer Ultimatums

THE ULMERS OF YORKTOWN were not your typical family.

The name derives from Ulm, a German city which is home to Ulmer Munster, the world's tallest cathedral. Three Ulmers—none closely related to those of our story—have achieved modest fame in America: film director Edgar, Keynesian economist Melville J., and jazz guitarist James "Blood."

The Ulmers were eventually to enjoy seven children, leading many to incorrectly assume Catholicism. Your writer was first-born. Five girls followed: Kathie, Kristine, Karen, Karol, and Karla. Mathematical odds of such an all-female succession are 32-to-1. Then, much later, came Mark.

The KKKKK of daughters' names was neither an extremist gesture like naming a boy Adolf nor an homage to a string of baseball strikeouts. Rather, "Kathie" commemorated Luther's wife, Katharina von Bora, and the K's just continued from there—a milder version of boxer George Foreman naming each of his several sons George.

When the Ulmers arrived in Yorktown in 1957 only "Dickie," Kathie and "Teenie" existed. Dickie soon insisted the diminutive "ie" be dropped, and Kristine so despised "Teenie" she has remained "Kris" since childhood. Karen was born in Yorktown (actually, the Clarinda hospital) in 1960, Karol in 1962, and Karla in 1964.

Beyond sheer size, the family fell outside other local norms as well. Unlike the rest of Yorktown's children, we were not allowed to trick-or-treat on Halloween—it was considered "begging." Nor were fireworks permitted on July 4th; one of Dad's childhood acquaintances had placed a "dud" firecracker in his mouth to grisly effect. Ulmers compensated by distributing "May baskets" on May 1. Crafted from pastel cupcake papers and colored pipe cleaners, these baskets were filled with candy, nuts, and violets, and then silently left on friends' doorsteps.

Yorktown

Ulmers did not eat what other Yorktownians ate. No white bread or white sugar passed our lips; instead, wheat bread and brown sugar. Potato chips and pop (excepting 7-Up for medicinal purposes) were banned from the home. No Yorktown Ulmer ever drank coffee. An early devotee of Julia Child, Mom amazed neighbors by whipping up cheese soufflés.

Cigarettes were verboten in the Ulmer household at a time when other Americans were sucking them down at an unprecedented rate. Play guns were forbidden as well. While other Yorktown kids plinked sparrows with BB guns, we tossed small green apples, becoming talented enough to knock a robin from its perch at twenty yards. Then one Christmas a pair of cap-gun six-shooters appeared under the tree. Why was never explained.

For most of their decade in Yorktown, the Ulmers defied mores by harboring no pets. It was felt the house already held enough mouths to feed. Then, in another inexplicable parental lapse, we acquired a Shetland pony named Licorice. His name was the only sweet thing about Licorice. He bit, bucked, and brayed. Neighbor Don Berringer, the local horse-whisperer, tried his luck to no avail. Three attempts to ride Licorice bareback left Don twisting on the ground. Finally, he jammed fingers into the recalcitrant pony's nostrils and forced a bit into his mouth. Still, Licorice soon sold at a loss.

The Ulmers were also noteworthy for having no television set or air conditioning. Dad considered television "the boob tube" and invested instead in a World Book Encyclopedia set. Every volume was repeatedly read cover to cover. Air conditioning was a frivolity—the pioneers had gotten by without it. This ended one steamy Iowa summer when Mom, pregnant yet again, demanded both TV and AC.

Traveling vacations were a joy experienced only vicariously via the new TV. The farthest we ventured was Pioneer Park, three miles distant on Highway 2. There, a Coleman camp stove warmed Spam or salami slices and baked beans. A Coleman lamp required an engineering degree to light. We also ate Kobey's—dried shoestring potatoes formed from the same ingredients as potato chips. Q: Why were the former permissible for Ulmer consumption, but not the latter? A: A false consistency is the hobgoblin of small minds.

That aphorism was proved anew by a sudden announcement that the Ulmers would be renting a trailer and grandly touring South Dakota, Colorado, and Kansas. First stop: the Corn Palace, a building covered entirely with colorful kernels of Indian corn in Mitchell, South Dakota.

Famous American sights fall into two categories: even-cooler-than-anticipated (Golden Gate Bridge, Statue of Liberty, Grand Canyon), and not-all-that-cool

(Liberty Bell, Hollywood, Florida coast). Our next stop, Mount Rushmore in the Black Hills, epitomizes the former. However, the high point of The First, Last, and Only Ulmer Family Vacation was "The World's Largest, Free, Outdoor, Municipal, Concrete Swimming Pool" in Garden City, Kansas.

CHAPTER 17

In a Strange Land

BOTH ULMER PARENTS GREW UP on the South Side of Chicago. Dad portrayed himself as a ragamuffin hawking newspapers on frozen street corners. Both parents also graduated from the Concordia teachers college in a Chicago suburb. The Lutheran call system then transported them to an alien environment: the rural Midwest.

Dad was not an immediate fit for small-town life. He had never handled, much less owned, a firearm. When we went fishing—once, at Pioneer Park—he could not unhook a blue gill, felt badly for the fish, and summarily abandoned the entire venture. He might tip a rare glass of wine, but never beer. He played third base for the Clarinda Legion fast-pitch softball team. However, when other players repaired to the local VFW for barley pop after a game, we instead visited A&W for thimble-size "baby beers." To promote cheering, A&W trips occurred only after victories.

In summer, Dad supplemented his teaching income as a surveyor for the federal government. He measured a cornfield and spray-painted a yellow mark on a fence; the farmer was paid for not growing corn past the mark. While surveying, Dad wore a Dr. Livingston-style pith helmet that branded him a city slicker. His excuse: not being a farmer, he lacked access to free seed caps.

Over time, however, Dad adapted to country ways. He superintended a vast garden of radishes, onions, lettuce, tomatoes, sweet corn, potatoes, and strawberries. A prized black-and-white photograph has him proudly hoisting a huge cabbage.

The family vehicle was a gray 1955 Chrysler Windsor given as a gift by a well-to-do Chicago relative. Nicknamed "Betsy" (like Dan'l Boone's rifle), the car boasted a V-8 engine and gray terrycloth seat covers intended to maintain resale value. Dad enjoyed driving a carload of kids through a town like Clarinda with traffic lights—to which we were little accustomed, as Yorktown had none. Waving his hands as though casting a spell, he incanted

"Change, light!" to "make" the signal turn green. That he peeked at the yellow for a perpendicular direction dawned on us only much later.

Dad also employed his own language, a version of pig Latin that Mom ostensibly could understand but not speak. A sampling: "Eezer kidsr gebezer." The language directed covert parental operations while children were present. The code never cracked.

Being American-made in the 1950s, Betsy's mechanical wellbeing was a constant concern. Dad further worried that "such an expensive car" sent the wrong message to St. Paul's parishioners, who drove pedestrian Fords and Chevys. It would not do for the Ulmers to be seen as big-headed.

CHAPTER 18

Hamburger 100 Ways

IN TRUTH, WE WERE POOR. St. Paul-Yorktown never paid "Teacher Ulmer" more than $5,000 a year—a pittance even in the 1960s. The rationalizations: teaching was not year-round work, a church-owned house called "the teacherage" provided free lodging, and farmer-congregants sometimes dropped off packages of meat from Mac's. Dad made ends meet with his summer surveying and toil on hay-baling crews.

Hamburger a hundred ways was Mom's culinary specialty. She also utilized other low-cost items more difficult to find on store shelves today. Velveeta was a "processed cheese product" foil-wrapped in a cardboard box. Most grocers do not bother to keep it under refrigeration. Velveeta was especially tasty atop homemade cinnamon rolls. Carnation Instant Milk was dried granules reconstituted with water. Oleomargarine substituted for butter.

Every family meal kicked off with the same prayer—"Come Lord Jesus be our guest and let thy gifts to us be blessed"—rendered in a single breath in nanoseconds. Likewise, failure to eat at ultrasonic speed meant no second helpings. At meal's end, we'd often sing: "One, two, three, four; who are we for? Momma, Momma, she's a good cook!"

Ulmers went out to eat—at Clarinda's Coachmen Inn—only when Grandma McClaughry treated while visiting from Chicago. Grandma Ulmer, who'd moved to Kansas City, was less well off than her counterpart, but happier. She played the "St. Louis Blues" on piano. ("Bring another round for the boys in the back," she'd call while pounding the keys.) Grandma Ulmer also snuck Salems in the bathroom, covering her indiscretion with bursts of heavy perfume.

Not uncommonly for the era, both grandfathers died in their early 50s. Both weighed too much, ate the wrong things, and never exercised. Our lone memories of Grandpa Ulmer had him (a) lustily singing "The Bear

Went Over the Mountain," beer in hand, and (b) standing waist-deep in a Kansas swimming pool, stogie in mouth. In Chicago, Grandpa McClaughry would furtively motion with a bent finger for an illicit trip to the ice cream shop in his finned white Cadillac.

Ulmer penny-pinching extended beyond food. Mom sewed many of our clothes. One Butterick pattern and a bolt of fabric produced dresses for all five girls. Haircuts were homemade too. Clippers on their lowest setting and pink "butch wax" created a crewcut. "The heat" from the furnace was kept low; children huddled around floor ducts on winter mornings. Baseball cards came off the backs of Jell-o and cereal boxes, because the kind packaged with chewing gum were too costly.

The teacherage had blond furniture in the Danish Modern style. Mom possessed a precious few knick-knacks; she called them "nice things." When we broke them, she would cry.

Corporal punishment was rare, but not unknown. One spring, the girls muddied new patent leather shoes just days before Easter by tracking through mud puddles. Ruination of such costly purchases was inexcusable. Mom lined up their bare bottoms on a bed and held forth with a yardstick. Laughter from the family's sole male child earned him addition to the row. Mom was the family disciplinarian because she was made of sterner stuff than Dad. When she tried to delegate spanking duty to him, he would take the offending child to another room, slap his hands together and tell the child to howl in pain. No one was fooled.

In addition to valuing shoes due to their cost, Mom demanded that they be worn indoors. Shoed feet might be needed in the event of an unspecified "emergency," she insisted.

As common for place and time, the words "love you" never passed between parent and child. Conventional Lutheran wisdom had it that actions spoke louder than words. And as a matter of fact, not all of us were lovable.

The Yorktown family's only boy in particular had a sadistic streak. In summer, while picking strawberries in the garden, he pelted sisters with rotten fruit. In winter, he swooped from behind to grab their looped sled runners and flip them over. After sledding one day, Kathie was convinced to lick a frozen runner. The sled had to be carried carefully home, tongue still firmly attached, where warm water was applied to free most of it.

While visiting Chicago one summer, Dad thought Betsy the Chrysler had expired on Detroit's designed timetable. (In fact, she lived several more years in the Windy City, piloted by an uncle.) A Plymouth station wagon followed. Unlike Betsy, the Plymouth had a cigarette lighter. This time, frequent foil Kathie was convinced to activate the lighter button and insert an index finger. Upon removal, her finger smoked like a pistol.

The mayhem, however, was not all one-way. When parents were out, Ulmer sisters pinned their brother to the floor—one atop each limb—and took turns expectorating in his face.

CHAPTER 19

Tornado!

Two forces in perpetual opposition create Iowa weather. Warm, humid Gulf of Mexico winds meet cool, drier fronts flowing over the Rocky Mountains. When the two collide in spring and summer, thunderstorms and tornadoes break out.

Tornados are far and away the most feared natural disaster in Southwest Iowa. Spring also brings occasional floods, but those affect only folks foolhardy enough to build in a floodplain. Winter blizzards just mean a day or two off from school.

A tornado begins with an invisible, horizontal spinning effect in the lower atmosphere. This gets tilted vertically into towering clouds, causing the storm to swirl and send funnels to ground. Winds in the funnel vortex can reach 250 mph and flatten everything in the tornado's path.

In Southwest Iowa, as elsewhere in tornado country, twisters have their own mythology. It is not true that trailer parks attract tornadoes; it only seems so because trailers offer such slim protection when a storm strikes. Nor are tornadoes repelled by bodies of water such as lakes or rivers. Another supposed myth is that one should open a house's windows when a tornado approaches to "equalize the pressure" and thereby minimize damage. In actuality, opening windows only allows winds to enter a house and wreck more havoc—or so experts claim.

The region of most frequent tornadoes is Tornado Alley. Beginning in Texas, it extends northeast through Oklahoma, Kansas, and northwest Missouri. Its northern tip: Page County, Iowa—and Yorktown.

April 12, 1964, was a sultry Sunday in Yorktown, unseasonably warm. We spent early afternoon watching high school kids play pickup basketball at St. Paul School, and then took a few spins on the merry-go-round. It looked like rain, so we headed home and curled up with a Hardy Boys mystery.

Yorktown

As so often happens before deadly disasters, the animals knew first. A horse in a fenced lot across the street inexplicably whinnied and ran wildly in circles. Soon the sky turned dark in a sickly shade of pea green. It was 4:30 P.M. We never saw the tornado coming.

In the 1960s Midwest, houses had "storm windows," attached outside regular windows for winter and replaced with screen windows come summer. These storm windows began to peel off and fly away. The house's all-weather front door bore a glass etching of the Battleship Maine, sinking of which started the Spanish-American War. A storm door was just outside that. Seconds later, the storm door ripped from its hinges and gyrated across the porch. We did not stay to see the Maine go down. Too late to open windows to "equalize pressure," we sprinted for the basement. Heedless of Mom's teaching, all children were shoeless.

Most tornadoes approach from the southwest. Thus a heavy wooden workbench is situated in that corner of many Midwestern basements. According to theory, even if a house is destroyed, deadly debris will fly away from people huddled under the bench, sparing them.

Tornado survivors often report "the sound of a thousand freight trains" passing over them. So here. Through the roar, we also heard a thumping as if malevolent children were jumping on the floor above us.

It was all over within a couple minutes, though it seemed an eternity. We climbed basement stairs and gazed up to see sky where roof had been. In stocking feet we could go no farther. "This is what happens when you kids don't wear your shoes in the house," Mom said, nodding knowingly.

CHAPTER 20

The Aftermath

HALF THE BUILDINGS IN Yorktown were destroyed. Essentially all suffered significant damage. Strangely, some of the least-substantial structures took the lightest hits. One person was dead—widowed grandmother Flora Eichhorst, found among remains of her obliterated house on the north side of town. Otherwise, only minor injuries.

Late to cover, neighbor Don Berringer saw the tornado hit the Ulmer teacherage. The house's outside walls expanded twice, as if inhaling and exhaling deep breaths. Then, on third expansion, the roof spun skyward as though expelled by a cough. This apparently "equalized pressure" that the closed windows could not. (So much for the experts.) The thumping we'd heard was falling chimney bricks left behind as the roof achieved liftoff.

The detached garage housing Betsy the Chrysler had disappeared. Concrete blocks were beneath her, but somehow she suffered only minor surface damage. Other oddities abounded. North of town near Highway 2, a grandmother was found sitting safely in her rocking chair in the middle of a cornfield, transported there by the tornado. An elderly farm couple south of town levitated down a flight of stairs, but were unharmed. Pieces of straw were driven into wood as if nails. Wooden boards stuck up from streets like porcupine quills.

Early the morning after, a hundred hammers rang out. Many were wielded by Mennonites (an Amish-lite religious sect) from eastern Iowa who'd traveled all night to render aid. Their flat hats and Lincoln-style beards in a town where men were normally clean-shaven made the scene all the more surreal. The National Guard, Salvation Army, and Red Cross soon arrived.

Mac's store was gone. Eichhorsts' too. The building housing the Tom Mix posters? Gone. The fence post that served as landmark for the buried silver dollar? Gone, treasure never to be relocated. In days that followed, the

Eichhorsts decided to close shop for good and move to Clarinda. But then Mac announced he would rebuild his store. Others followed. Yorktown lived!

Omaha TV newsman Lee Terry—famed for "commie fighter" editorials—hosted a half-hour documentary, "Yorktown: Too Tough To Die." (Terry went on to represent Omaha in the U.S. House of Representatives, and his eponymous son holds the seat today.)

Yorktown, the place where nothing ever happened, was suddenly on the map. All summer, lookie loos from Highway 2 cruised town to survey damage. This grew wearisome, so Yorktown children made rude faces at them.

Another tornado myth is that once a locale is hit by a twister it will never be struck again. Not so. In July 1964, Dad insisted on loading up the family for a softball game in Shenandoah, though ominous skies threatened. Emotionally scarred, we warned another tornado was imminent.

Within a few miles, funnels danced down from the clouds. Chasing Betsy, they threw up debris. The preferred alternative in this predicament is to abandon one's vehicle and lie flat in a deep roadside ditch, hoping and praying the twister will pass over. The Ulmers instead elected to successfully race the funnels back to Yorktown.

In September 1964, myth was busted yet again when a third tornado ripped off a barn door just south of town.

CHAPTER 21

Too Tough to Die?

YORKTOWN MADE HEADLINES of a sort again two years later. On April 23, 1966, a farmer just outside town reported a UFO landing at 2:10 A.M. Aliens lacking in creativity, the object took the usual "cigar shape." "Blood red" light bathed the area as the UFO rested on "seventeen to twenty long legs." The farmer, being a farmer, simply made his observations and returned to bed.

At about this same time, the Ulmers moved to the big city of Omaha, thus diminishing Yorktown's population by almost 5 percent. Dad had been called by another, larger Lutheran school. After that, we passed through Yorktown on occasional road trips. Distressingly, the 1949 penny had disappeared from the St. Paul School flagpole by the early 1980s. Worse was to come.

The family—now including many grandchildren anxious to see the Yorktown of lore—visited *en masse* in June 2002. St. Paul Church was gone—burned to the ground in 1998 under mysterious circumstances. Hellish tongues of flame lick from church windows in photos of the event. The Lutherans built a new sanctuary northeast of Yorktown on Highway 2. The Methodist church was gone too, replaced by a ramshackle civic park. Mac had died in 1987; the post office was later slated for closure.

St. Paul School was closed—combined with former rival Immanuel in a new Lutheran school in Clarinda. The forlorn school building, converted to living quarters, was surrounded by a fence pasturing horses and ponies. A small Shetland lay dead on the former school's front lawn, flies buzzing around its glazed eyes. Watching from shadows was a silent wanderer of the 1960s. Sixty-something now, he still wore a long-sleeved buttoned-up work shirt just as forty years earlier. At least *he* hadn't changed.

Yorktown's 2010 census actually showed a 4 percent increase from 2000—eighty-two residents to eighty-five. But this was no revitalization. No one ran for mayor in the November 2011 election, and only two write-in votes were cast. Both "winners" told the *Omaha World-Herald* they did not want the position. "Should this be a town that should become unincorporated?" asked a Page County official—a query made all the more biting by her grand old Yorktown name: Melissa Wellhausen.

Would apathy finally kill the town "too tough to die"?

Postscript

RICHARD ULMER SR. CONTINUED as principal of St. Paul Lutheran School in Omaha until retirement. Marian Ulmer went back to teaching, at St. Paul-Omaha, after her children were largely grown. All six of the couple's living children, all 12 grandchildren, and many significant others celebrated the 80th birthdays of "G&G" (Grandma and Grandpa) with a three-day extravaganza in July 2011.

One more child, Mark, was born after the move to Omaha. His nativity made international news (newspaper clippings arrived from as far away as the Philippines). This was because it occurred so soon after

Postscript

Mom's toboggan ride to the hospital through a raging blizzard. Mark died in 1986 after a long battle with leukemia.

Today, Kathie Wolfert is an award-winning registered nurse at Nebraska Methodist Hospital in Omaha. Her visage has appeared on the hospital's jumbo Interstate 80 billboard.

Kris Hock attended Benson High School in Omaha (as did all siblings save Mark)—a school topped by an historic cupola. As a senior, Kris was voted "Girl You'd Most Like to Be Locked Up in the Cupola With." She is now a fourth-grade teacher at Bethlehem Lutheran School in suburban Denver.

Karen Samson operates a house-cleaning business in Omaha and is renowned as an interior decorator. Siblings have finished marathons and half-marathons, but Karen runs most religiously.

Karol Ulmer is a business systems consultant at Mutual of Omaha. Living in the city's leafy Dundee neighborhood, Karol recently bought the house next door and renovated it top to bottom. She's now scouting for the next "flipping" project.

Karla Haggar is a nursing coordinator for the University of Nebraska Medical Center. Karla is also a regional vice president for Arbonne International, an outfit her big brother derided as a "pyramid scheme" until she e-mailed to ask what color her Arbonne-awarded Mercedes should be.

Acknowledgements

THANK YOU TO PAUL R. SARRETT of Auburn, California. His online article "A Town Too Tough to Die" provided detail of early Yorktown events.

Thanks also to the Rev. Nathan Dudley, current pastor of St. Paul Lutheran Church-Yorktown, for sharing materials about the church's history.

About the Author

RICHARD B. ("DICK") ULMER JR. attended Benson High School in Omaha, where he wrote a column, "Ulmer's Ultimatums," for the school newspaper. He studied journalism and history at the University of Nebraska at Omaha, graduating with honors. Dick worked as a reporter for ten years—at the *Omaha Sun* (the first newspaper Warren Buffett purchased), then the *Lincoln Journal-Star* (where he roamed back roads of Nebraska writing feature stories), and finally the *Omaha World-Herald*, the region's largest newspaper.

After writing the day-after-Thanksgiving-shopping story for the third year in a row, Dick decided to try law

About the Author

school. He graduated from Stanford Law in 1986, again with honors, and then worked as a civil litigator in the San Francisco Bay Area for twenty-three years. His final position was as a partner in the Silicon Valley office of Latham & Watkins, where he tried complex contract, trade secret, and patent cases for clients such as Genentech, Adobe, and Apple. Dick also led a decade-long pro bono effort to reform conditions in the California Youth Authority, the state's prison system for juveniles, as well as county juvenile halls. California Governor Arnold Schwarzenegger appointed Dick a Superior Court judge in San Francisco in 2009. Months later, a faction of the Democratic Party opposed to Schwarzenegger tried to depose Judge Ulmer in an election. Though Democrats outnumber Republicans eight to one in the city, Dick won the election in November 2010 at the same time his beloved San Francisco Giants won the World Series for the first time.

Dick and his wife, Anita Stork, a partner at the Covington & Burling law firm, have one daughter, Rikki, a freshman at Tulane University in New Orleans.

Made in the USA
Columbia, SC
20 February 2025